Georgia Bulldogs IQ: The Ultimate Test of True Fandom

Keith Gaddie & Kim Gaddie

IQ Series books are the trademark of Black Mesa Publishing, LLC.

Cataloging-in-Publication Data is available from the Library of Congress.

ISBN: 1449558046
First edition, first printing

Cover photo by Keith Gaddie

Black Mesa Publishing, LLC
Florida
David Horne and Marc CB Maxwell
Black.Mesa.Publishing@gmail.com

Contents

Introduction

Think you know Georgia Bulldogs Football? Think again. In this brand new book in the IQ Sports Series find out how smart you really are about the Dawgs. Anybody can tailgate, but can you make it through the whole game, playing under the hot Georgia sun, grinding it out on the red clay of Sanford Stadium against Auburn? Will you earn that cool drink that tastes of success and hear the peal of the Chapel Bell marking yet another victory?

We'll let you know.

Test your skills. Wrack your brain. It's the ultimate Georgia Bulldogs IQ test.

Seven chapters, more than 250 questions – that's what you're up against, and we're keeping score.

We start with the Pregame Tailgate – just some light tailgating and a little bit of stretching before the game starts.

Afterwards, it's kickoff time – the First Quarter of the big game. If you're up for the challenge then it'll be on to the Second Quarter.

You'll catch a break at Half Time.

And with some luck, your mad trivia skills will be just good enough to get you back out on the field to start the Third Quarter.

If you find success there, well, then you'll be on the field when it counts the most – out in the trenches during the Fourth Quarter, the game on the line, the crowd cheering you on, the fate of the season resting entirely upon your ability to seal the deal.

And if you can do that, well, we're still not quite done with you – because you'll have one last test you must face before you get any accolades from us.

We call it: "Meaner Than a Junkyard Dawg." And that sums it up pretty well, don't you think?

So here we go . . . the grills are fired up, the bourbon and coke is mixed in your stadium cup, and 93,000 of your best friends are hanging out under an old oak near the cemetery by Baldwin Hall, ready to walk over to Sanford Stadium. There's a game about to start, and you'll want to be there for kickoff!

Keith & Kim Gaddie
Sitting on the dock at Lake Burton, Georgia, waiting for Fall to come

Chapter One

PRE-GAME TAILGATE

QUESTION 1: Suppose you stopped at the Georgia Bar on west Clayton Street and got a beer and some peanuts before the game. How far would your walk be to the stadium?

QUESTION 2: Who is the Sanford in Sanford Stadium?

QUESTION 3: How many Ugas have there been?

QUESTION 4: Who won the first Georgia-Auburn game, on February 20, 1892?

QUESTION 5: What was the first UGA team to go undefeated in SEC play?

QUESTION 6: Can you name three Bulldogs who have been overall #1 picks in the NFL draft?

QUESTION 7: True or false: Vince Dooley had a winning record against Auburn as head coach at UGA.

QUESTION 8: Which of the following is something Herschel Walker did not do?
   a) Compete in the Olympic bobsled event
   b) Hold the world record for the 60-meter dash
   c) Compete in the Ultimate Fighting League
   d) Dance with the Dallas Ballet

QUESTION 9: Which Uga appeared on the cover of *Sports Illustrated* as the best mascot in college sports?

QUESTION 10: One Bulldog head coach is undefeated in bowl game play, winning every bowl game he coached with the Red and Black.   Who is the undefeated postseason Bulldog coach?
   a) Jim Donnan
   b) Ray Goff
   c) Mark Richt
   d) Wally Butts

QUESTION 11: When Sanford Stadium was originally constructed in 1929, it seated 30,000. About how many students went to UGA at the time?
   a) 10,000
   b) 5,000
   c) 8,000
   d) 2,000

QUESTION 12: Before it came into the SEC, UGA was part of the Southern Intercollegiate Athletic Association. How many conference titles did the Dawgs win in the SIAA? Who were the coaches?

QUESTION 13: In the first football game in UGA history, the Red and Black scored 50 points against Mercer in Athens. The game, witnessed by numerous hometown fans and also about 200 visitors from Macon, featured the first pregame tailgate in Georgia history. Where exactly was the game played?

QUESTION 14: On September 19, 1964, Lewis Grizzard covered his first Georgia game as a journalist –

freshman Grizzard was hired by WAGA's Ed Thilenius to act as spotter on the opposing team. It was also Vince Dooley's first game as head coach at UGA. They played Alabama in Tuscaloosa. What happened?

QUESTION 15: "Mr. Bulldog," Herschel Scott of Monroe, attended more consecutive UGA games than any other fan. The streak started in 1962, and Scott died years later after a particularly bad loss to an SEC opponent. He lost hundreds of dollars to kids with his favorite bet, asking "Hey, kid, I'll give you a quarter if you can name the greatest football team in the world!" How many games was his attendance streak?

QUESTION 16: How many sky suites are there in Sanford Stadium?
  a) 33
  b) 77
  c) 88
  d) 126

QUESTION 17: Where are "the seats that Herschel built"?

QUESTION 18: Follow-up: How many seats are there? What year were they built? And what more-famous seats did they replace (displace)?

QUESTION 19: What's the actual name of the original Uga?
  a) Hood's Ole Dan
  b) Ole Dan's Uga
  c) Whatchagot Loran
  d) Wally's Butts

QUESTION 20: What is the only Uga to never go to a Sugar Bowl?
    a) Uga I
    b) Uga II
    c) Uga V
    d) Uga VI

QUESTION 21: One UGA head coach is undefeated at Sanford Stadium. Who is it?

QUESTION 22: On September 17, 1965, Vince Dooley's Dawgs would stun defending national champion Alabama 18-17, in a nationally-televised game on ABC. It was Vince Dooley's first coaching victory over Bear Bryant. What is the other notable first of this game?

QUESTION 23: Who was Georgia's coach in 1896? He was paid $480 for the season.

QUESTION 24: What was the nickname of the undefeated 1939 freshman Georgia Bullpups team, which featured future stars Lamar "Racehorse" Davis and Frank Sinkwich?

QUESTION 25: True or False: UGA has never been shut out in a bowl game?

QUESTION 26: How many times have the Dawgs won the SEC but not played in the Sugar Bowl?

QUESTION 27: True or false: The undefeated Georgia Bulldogs ran fewer offensive plays than their opponents in 1980.

QUESTION 28: Who was the leading rusher for the first-ever Vince Dooley-coached Bulldog team?

QUESTION 29: What was the first endorsement deal that Herschel Walker got after he went pro?

QUESTION 30: Which team had a better yards-per-carry rushing average – the 2007 Georgia Bulldogs or the 1980 Bulldogs?

Chapter One Answer Key

Time to find out how you did – put a check mark next to the questions you answered correctly, and when you are done be sure and add up your score. You'll need it after the final chapter to find out your Bulldogs IQ!

___ **QUESTION 1:** It measures 1,891 yards, which is the same as the distance rushed by Herschel Walker in 1981.

___ **QUESTION 2:** Steadman Vincent Stanford, dean of the University of Georgia. He pushed forward with the construction of a 30,000 seat stadium in a city of 15,000 to make Georgia Tech and other national powers come to Athens to play football.

___ **QUESTION 3:** Seven.

___ **QUESTION 4:** Auburn, 12-0.

___ **QUESTION 5:** Wally Butts' 1948 team went 6-0-0.

___ **QUESTION 6:** Charlie Trippi (1947); Harry Babcock (1953); Matthew Stafford (2009).

___ **QUESTION 7:** False. Dooley was 11-13-1 against Auburn, including 6-6-0 against his mentor (and former UGA assistant) Shug Jordan.

___ **QUESTION 8:** C – Compete in the Ultimate Fighting League.

___ **QUESTION 9:** Uga V.

___ **QUESTION 10:** A – Jim Donnan.

___ **QUESTION 11:** D – 2,000.

___ **QUESTION 12:** Two, in 1896 with Pop Warner and in 1920 under Herman Stegeman.

___ **QUESTION 13:** Herty Field, north campus.

___ **QUESTION 14:** Alabama won the game 31-3 and also the national championship.

___ **QUESTION 15:** It was 471 games, ending with a loss in 2003 – and if you want to know which SEC opponent beat UGA that day, keep reading . . .

___ **QUESTION 16:** B – 77.

___ **QUESTION 17:** Upper deck, east end zone.

___ **QUESTION 18:** There are 19,000 seats that Herschel built. The east end zone was bowled for the 1981 season. The new seats displaced the seats of the Railroad Track people, the frat boys who dragged sofas onto the railroad bridge and cheered on the Dawgs and berated the opposition.

___ **QUESTION 19:** A – Hood's Ole Dan.

___ **QUESTION 20:** C – Uga V.

___ **QUESTION 21:** Joel Hunt, head coach in 1938. Hunt went 3-0-1 at home and then left UGA. Assistant Wally Butts took over.

___ **QUESTION 22:** It was the first nationally-televised game from Sanford Stadium.

___ **QUESTION 23:** Pop Warner.

___ **QUESTION 24:** The "point-a-minute-freshmen."

___ **QUESTION 25:** True. The fewest points ever scored by the Dawgs in a bowl game: *two* – in the 1969 Sugar Bowl against Arkansas.

___ **QUESTION 26:** Four times (the Dawgs have a dozen SEC championships but played in eight subsequent Sugar Bowls.)

___ **QUESTION 27:** True. Georgia had fewer ball snaps (766) than its opponents (787).

___ **QUESTION 28:** Preston Ridelhuber who led Dooley's first two Bulldog teams in rushing with 368 and 401 yards respectively.

___ **QUESTION 29:** The McDonald's "Big Mac Attack."

___ **QUESTION 30:** Georgia had a 4.53 yard-per-carry average in 2007, or about two inches per carry better than the 1980 team.

Got your Tailgating total? ___ / 30
Good luck in the First Quarter!

Chapter Two

FIRST QUARTER

QUESTION 1: Which Uga was the *fattest*?

QUESTION 2: In the inaugural game at Sanford Stadium, Spud Chandler tossed the winning touchdown pass against Yale. For what team did UGA's great quarterback and sprinter of the 1920s play Major League baseball?

QUESTION 3: The first Georgia-Clemson game was in Athens on October 9, 1897. UGA won the game. What was the score?

QUESTION 4: In their first bowl game ever, the 1942 Orange Bowl, Georgia led by Frank Sinkwich scored 40 points on Texas Christian. What is the record for points scored by a Georgia team in a bowl game?

QUESTION 5: You probably know that Georgia played its first bowl game in the 1942 Orange Bowl, and that the Dawgs played Texas Christian. Do you know the halftime score?

QUESTION 6: What street did Sonny Seiler, the owner of the line of Ugas, live on while he was in law school and keeping Uga I?

QUESTION 7: When he was a second year law student, Judge Sonny Seiler, and his wife Cecelia received a white English Bulldog pup as a gift. They took the little pup to the UGA home game that weekend, on September 29, 1956, dressed in a little red Georgia jersey. Here begins the reign of Uga. Who was the game against? And who was the opposing halfback? What was the score of the game?

QUESTION 8: The first on-campus playing field for UGA was Herty Field, which was located on North Campus. If you headed from the Chapel toward the old Holiday Inn on Lumpkin, the green space you cross was once Herty Field. The Red and Black played there until 1920. The field was named for a chemistry professor, Charles Herty. Why?

QUESTION 9: Who were the "Dream and Wonder" Bulldogs?

QUESTION 10: How much did the original Sanford Stadium cost?

QUESTION 11: How was it paid for?

QUESTION 12: What's the name of the guy who flies the plane around the stadium towing the advertising banners?

QUESTION 13: What kind of hedge is the hedge around the playing field at Sanford Stadium?

QUESTION 14: Who suggested the idea of putting in the hedges back in 1928?

QUESTION 15: Who won the first Georgia-Auburn game, on February 20, 1892?

QUESTION 16: Who was the first Korean-American to be All-SEC at UGA?

QUESTION 17: Do the Bulldogs have a winning record in televised games decided by only one-score?

QUESTION 18: What was the score of the first-ever Georgia-Auburn game, played in Atlanta on February 20, 1892?

QUESTION 19: On October 5, 1991, Georgia upset Clemson in Eric Zeier's first game of the season. The 27-12 victory between the hedges occurred amidst a surreal scene of Georgia Bulldogs doing the "tomahawk chop" and Seminole war chant from Florida State. Why did they do this?

QUESTION 20: The first time UGA played Georgia Tech was on November 4, 1893. Who won the game?

QUESTION 21: At the time of the first Georgia-Georgia Tech game, the schools were not known as the Bulldogs and the Yellow Jackets. What were the teams called?

QUESTION 22: The single-season record for tackles is 170, and the single-game record of 26 tackles is held by the same player. Who is he?

QUESTION 23: The record for total career PATs by a UGA kicker is 148. Who set it?
   a) Kanon Parkman
   b) Billy Bennett
   c) Kevin Butler

QUESTION 24: When was the first time the Georgia-Florida game was played in Gainesville?

QUESTION 25: The longest kickoff return ever by a Bulldog in a bowl game is 86 yards in the 2001 Music City Bowl. Who accomplished that feat?
  a) Champ Bailey
  b) David Greene
  c) Decory Bryant
  d) Hines Ward

QUESTION 26: The first Georgia-Florida game was won by UGA, 52-0. It was played on October 15, 1904, at a neutral site. Where was the game played?

QUESTION 27: In the 1981 Sugar Bowl, Herschel Walker was the only rusher to have positive yardage, averaging 4.17 yards per carry, 150 yards on 36 carries. What happened to Walker in the first quarter?

QUESTION 28: Who was the first Bulldog to rush for over 1,000 yards in a single season?
  a) Kevin McLee
  b) Herschel Walker
  c) Willie McClendon
  d) Frank Sinkwich

QUESTION 29: From 1980-82, Herschel Walker broke 1,000 yards rushing in three consecutive seasons. It was the first time individual Georgia running backs had rushed for 1,000 yards or more in three straight seasons. Three different backs subsequently pulled the trick off in consecutive seasons. Who were they?

QUESTION 30: Who was the first All-American back at the University of Georgia? Hint: He came from a small Georgia town and was known for his powerful thighs.
    a) Herschel Walker
    b) Bob McWhorter
    c) Bill Hartman
    d) George Patton

QUESTION 31: You know that the name of UGA's first Heisman Trophy winner was Frank Sinkwich, a halfback/quarterback who teamed up with Charley Trippi as the famous "Touchdown Twins" combo in 1942. What was Frank's other nickname?

QUESTION 32: A lot of fans know that the first game played at Sanford Stadium was against Yale in 1929. Catfish Smith scored all of Georgia's points in the upset of Yale. What was the score, and how much was a ticket for the game?

QUESTION 33: The career field goal percentage completion record is 80.8% (53 for 66). Who set the record?
    a) Kanon Parkman
    b) Kevin Butler
    c) Charley Trippi
    d) Brandon Coutu

QUESTION 34: Lights were installed in Sanford Stadium in 1940. Georgia and Kentucky tied in that first game, 7-7. Who was the quarterback for the Dawgs that day?

QUESTION 35: How long was Herschel Walker's rush the first time he touched a ball in a UGA game? Bonus points: who did he run over?

QUESTION 36: Georgia and Virginia have played a total of 19 games since 1897. Georgia leads the series 9-7-3 and they last played in the Oahu bowl. The first game is remembered for a very different reason, involving a player named Von Gammons. What did Von Gammons do on his last play of the game?

QUESTION 37: Harry Mehre was UGA's coach in the first game at Sanford Stadium, a 15-0 win over mighty Yale on October 12, 1929. He also coached the first loss just three weeks later, to the Tulane Green Wave. Overall, Mehre never won the SEC or was sent to a bowl game. Was he a winning coach at home?

QUESTION 38: Since moving to Jacksonville in 1933, the series record of the Georgia-Florida game stands at 37-37-1. It is one of the most hotly-contested rivalries in football. What share of games since 1964 are decided by less than one score?
   a) A quarter
   b) A third
   c) Half
   d) Two thirds

QUESTION 39: The longest pass play in the history of the Bulldogs was 67 yards, in the 1947 Sugar Bowl against North Carolina. All-American Charley Trippi threw the pass. The guy who caught it was a first round NFL pick who played in the NFL. Name the receiver.

QUESTION 40: The record for points scored by one UGA player in a bowl game is 18, set by Rodney Hampton. What bowl game did he set the record in?
   a) Gator Bowl
   b) Peach Bowl
   c) Sugar Bowl

Chapter Two Answer Key

Time to find out how you did – put a check mark next to the questions you answered correctly, and when you are done be sure and add up your score. You'll need it after the final chapter to find out your Bulldogs IQ!

___ **QUESTION 1:** Uga VI.

___ **QUESTION 2:** The New York Yankees.

___ **QUESTION 3:** 24-0.

___ **QUESTION 4:** The record is 41, scored on the Hawaii Rainbow Warriors in the 2008 Sugar Bowl.

___ **QUESTION 5:** It was 33-7, Georgia.

___ **QUESTION 6:** Morningside Drive, which is two blocks off of Baxter Street, behind the dorms.

___ **QUESTION 7:** Florida State. Lee Corso. 3-0, Bulldogs.

___ **QUESTION 8:** Charles Herty organized the first UGA football team.

___ **QUESTION 9:** The 1927 Bulldogs who went 9-1-0 and defeated Yale in New Haven, and staked a claim to a part of the National Title.

___ **QUESTION 10:** $360,000.

___ **QUESTION 11:** A bank loan paid for by alums and fans in exchange for lifetime seats.

___ **QUESTION 12:** Tommy Lenhart, who flies out of Jackson County Airport.

___ **QUESTION 13:** An English Privit hedge.

___ **QUESTION 14:** The UGA athletic department's Charlie Morton.

___ **QUESTION 15:** Auburn.

___ **QUESTION 16:** Hines Ward, 1997. Ward was born in Seoul.

___ **QUESTION 17:** Yes. The Dawgs are 53-35-5 with a 59.6% winning percentage in televised, one-score games.

___ **QUESTION 18:** It was 12-0, Auburn.

___ **QUESTION 19:** The Atlanta Braves clinched the NL West that day.

___ **QUESTION 20:** Tech won 28-6, thanks to a ringer, Dr. Leonard Wood. Georgia fans chased the Tech team down College Avenue to the train station, throwing rocks. This initial experience inspired the rivalry's nickname, "Clean, Old-Fashioned Hate." The rivalry was not renewed for another four years.

___ **QUESTION 21:** Tech was called the Blacksmiths and UGA the Red and Black.

___ **QUESTION 22:** Linebacker Knox Culpepper (1984).

___ **QUESTION 23:** B – Billy Bennett.

___ **QUESTION 24:** It was 1931. Coach Harry Mehre's Bulldogs spoiled the Gators homecoming with a 33-6 win.

___ **QUESTION 25:** C – Decory Bryant.

___ **QUESTION 26:** Macon.

___ **QUESTION 27:** He dislocated his shoulder.

___ **QUESTION 28:** C – Willie McClendon.

___ **QUESTION 29:** Lars Tate (1,016 yards in 1987); Tim Worley (1,216 yards in 1988); and Rodney Hampton (1,059 yards in 1989).

___ **QUESTION 30:** B – Bob McWhorter.

___ **QUESTION 31:** Flatfoot Frankie.

___ **QUESTION 32:** The Bulldogs of Georgia beat the Bulldogs of Yale 15-0. Seats were $3 apiece, or less than the cost of a Coke in Sanford Stadium.

___ **QUESTION 33:** D – Brandon Coutu.

___ **QUESTION 34:** Frank Sinkwich.

___ **QUESTION 35:** Sixteen yards. And he ran over Tennessee's Bill Bates, setting up a great Larry Munson call: "We hand it off to Herschel. There's a hole. Five, 10, 12. He's running over people. Oh, you Herschel Walker! My God almighty! He ran right through two men. Herschel ran right over two men. They had him dead away inside the nine. Herschel Walker went 16 yards. He drove right over orange shirts just driving and running with those big thighs. My God, a freshman!"

___ **QUESTION 36:** He got killed. The state legislature very nearly outlawed the game in the state until Gammons' mother interceded to ask the governor to veto the football ban bill.

___ **QUESTION 37:** Hell yes! Mehre was 25-7-2 at Sanford Stadium (76.5%).

___ **QUESTION 38:** C – Half.

___ **QUESTION 39:** Dan Edwards, who was the #9 pick in the 1948 draft by the Steelers.

___ **QUESTION 40:** A – Gator Bowl.

Got your First Quarter total? ___ / 40
Good luck in the Second Quarter!

Chapter Three

SECOND QUARTER

QUESTION 1: The Rose Bowl is the oldest bowl game in the country. Name the second-oldest bowl game in the country.

QUESTION 2: The second UGA was UGA II. The Dawgs went 42-16-3 in UGA II's brief six-year reign, but they won the SEC twice, grabbed part of one national title, and nearly won the whole shooting match another season except for a loss to the Miami Hurricanes. What date did UGA II take over from his namesake daddy?

QUESTION 3: The highest career total kickoff return yards is 1,669 total yards, 525 yards more than the next best return artist at UGA. Who ranks one and two, respectively, in return yards at UGA?
  a) Lindsay Scott and Gene Washington
  b) Gene Washington and Lindsay Scott
  c) Hines Ward and Lindsay Scott
  d) Gene Washington and Hines Ward

QUESTION 4: True or false: Herschel Walker is the only sophomore to rush for at least 1,000 yards as a sophomore at UGA.

QUESTION 5: Can you name the first two seasons Vince Dooley won the SEC with UGA?

QUESTION 6: Since the dawn of the modern college football era in 1945 through 2007, the University of

Georgia Bulldogs have a .668 winning percentage during the regular season, third best in the Southeastern Conference and 13th best all-time among all major football programs (the Dawgs are 474-215-19). What two SEC teams have better records since 1945?

QUESTION 7: Until 1981, the following rule was used to determine who went to the Sugar Bowl if there was a tie for the conference championship: the team that had not been to the Sugar Bowl most-recently got to go. The SEC and the Sugar Bowl saw fit to change this rule in 1981 when Alabama tied Georgia for the SEC title. Why, and to what rule?

QUESTION 8: In the last AP Poll of 1959, Georgia was ranked #5, as All-Americans Pat Dye and Francis Tarkenton led the Dawgs to a 10-1 record and the SEC championship. Two other SEC teams ranked ahead of UGA at the end of the season, and played each other in the Sugar Bowl. What teams?

QUESTION 9: Uga II took over in 1966, and stood on the sidelines for seven seasons. Uga II had his career cut short due to an unfortunate accident. What happened?

QUESTION 10: In the 1980 game at Jordan-Hare, Auburn shut down Herschel Walker and led 7-0 midway through the second quarter. Then, with seven minutes left in the half, Rex Robinson scored a field goal to put Georgia on the board. Seven plays later, Greg Bell blocked an Auburn punt and Freddie Gilbert recovered and ran it in for a 27-yard TD score. On Georgia's next possession, they got to the Auburn one and Buck passed to TE Norris Brown to score again as the half ended. An unsportsmanlike call was made against an Auburn assistant for running on the field, which was applied to UGA's kickoff to start the second half. Georgia risked an onside kick from the UGA 45, recovered on Auburn's 33, and Buck Belue ran the ball in for a TD to take a 24-7 lead. Who was the UGA offensive coordinator that made the gutsy onsides' kick call?

QUESTION 11: What was the primary offensive formation that Ray Goff ran in his two seasons as UGA's quarterback in 1975 and 1976?
  a) The Wishbone
  b) The Veer
  c) The Power I
  d) The Single Wing

QUESTION 12: Theron Sapp is one of two UGA halfbacks to score a dozen points in the Senior Bowl, pulling off the trick in 1959. Who is the other?
  a) Charley Trippi, 1946
  b) Fred Brown, 1960
  c) Kevin McLee, 1975

QUESTION 13: From 1980 to 1982, Herschel Walker rushed for at least 100 yards in a game 28 times, which is still a UGA record. Who is second on the list?

QUESTION 14: In 1997 senior RB Robert Edwards rushed for 908 yards and scored a dozen touchdowns. The Dawgs went 10-2 and Edwards' rushing was good enough for third all-time among UGA seniors. Name the two tailbacks that rank ahead of Edwards on the senior list.

QUESTION 15: Willie McClendon and his son Brandon McClendon both played for two of the same teams – can you name those two teams?

QUESTION 16: How many times has the Georgia-Florida game been played in Jacksonville, through 2009?

QUESTION 17: Who holds the UGA record for most tackles in a bowl game, with 15?
  a) Ben Zambiasi, 1976 Cotton Bowl
  b) Richard Tardits, 1989 Gator Bowl
  c) Bill Goldberg, 1989 Peach Bowl

QUESTION 18: The 1984 Citrus Bowl ended in 17-17 tie of FSU and Georgia, when Kevin Butler's game-ending field goal attempt came up a foot short. How long was the attempt?

QUESTION 19: Georgia has a 76.2% winning percentage against those other bulldogs down in Statesboro, Mississippi State University. UGA is 16-5-0 all-time. What is the name of Miss State's bulldog mascot?

QUESTION 20: True or false: Georgia has an all-time winning record at Auburn's Jordan-Hare Stadium.

QUESTION 21: Through 2009, the Georgia Bulldogs have been shut out 127 times in 1,150 games, or 11.04% of all games. When was the last time the Dawgs were shut out going into the 2009 season?

QUESTION 22: The UGA Bowl record for total offense (469 yards) was set in the 1995 Peach Bowl by what player?

QUESTION 23: There have been 112 games played in the Deep South's Oldest Rivalry with Auburn. What is UGA's record in those games?

QUESTION 24: At old Herty Field, the Dawgs were 4-2-0 against Tech. At Sanford Stadium, in 38 games the Dawgs have won 25 and lost 12 with one tie. The tie is the last tie to occur in the series. When was it?

QUESTION 25: How many points did Herschel Walker score in his Heisman Trophy season of 1982?

QUESTION 26: What Bulldog led the SEC in scoring in 2005, with 114 points?

QUESTION 27: The UGA all-time record for yards gained per play is 7.52 yards. Who holds the record? Hint: he played for the national title.
   a) Charley Trippi
   b) Herschel Walker
   c) Frank Sinkwich
   d) Buck Belue

QUESTION 28: How many records did Herschel Walker set on the field from 1980-82 that still stand?

QUESTION 29: The NCAA record for games by a kicker with at least one field goal is 43, and held by a Bulldog. Who is it?
   a) Charlie Trippi
   b) Kevin Butler
   c) Kanon Parkman
   d) Billy Butler

QUESTION 30: Who holds the UGA record for interceptions, with 16? He played college and pro ball with fellow Bulldog Bill Stanfill.

QUESTION 31: Wally Butts' autobiography was titled "No Ifs, No Ands, and a Whole Lot of Butts," published after he retired as head coach. Who wrote the book with him?

QUESTION 32: True or false: A Vince Dooley-coached team was never outscored for the season.

QUESTION 33: UGA started playing homecoming games in 1922. In 2006, UGA lost the homecoming game to Vanderbilt. When was the previous time Georgia lost to Vandy for homecoming?

QUESTION 34: Who is the last significant "iron man" in Georgia football history, playing both ways (cornerback, receiver) and on special teams?

QUESTION 35: In 21 years of coaching at UGA, Wally Butts won 140 games. Which of the following bowl games did Butts not win?
   a) Orange
   b) Rose
   c) Sugar
   d) Cotton

QUESTION 36: Pat Dye was an outstanding offensive lineman at UGA, and later coached East Carolina and Auburn. He won three SEC titles between 1983 and 1988, but was ousted in a scandal related to booster payments to players under his tenure. What was Pat's record against the Bulldogs as head coach at Auburn?

QUESTION 37: How many players other than Herschel Walker were involved in the famous "Herschel Walker Trade" of Herschel from the Dallas Cowboys to the Minnesota Vikings?
   a) four
   b) eight
   c) eleven
   d) sixteen

QUESTION 38: The record yards per carry in a single game by a Bulldog running back is 6.76 yards per carry. The record is held by a Vince Dooley running back, and the game was a UGA win over Auburn. Who holds the record?
   a) Kevin McLee
   b) Herschel Walker
   c) Lars Tate
   d) Willie McClendon

QUESTION 39: True or False: Herschel Walker averaged fewer yards in SEC road games than SEC home games.

QUESTION 40: Vince Dooley's career winning percentage at UGA was 71.5%. Dooley was 201-77-10 from 1964-88, with 20 bowl appearances, with a National Championship in 1980 – just in case you didn't know. Now, did Dooley have a winning record in bowl games at UGA?

Chapter Three Answer Key

Time to find out how you did – put a check mark next to the questions you answered correctly, and when you are done be sure and add up your score. You'll need it after the final chapter to find out your Bulldogs IQ!

___ **QUESTION 1:** The Sugar Bowl.

___ **QUESTION 2:** October 14, 1966.

___ **QUESTION 3:** B – Gene Washington and Lindsay Scott.

___ **QUESTION 4:** False. Knowshon Moreno also broke the 1,000 yard mark as a sophomore, in 2008.

___ **QUESTION 5:** 1966 and 1968.

___ **QUESTION 6:** Alabama and Tennessee.

___ **QUESTION 7:** Georgia had gone for Sugar the year before, but the Sugar Bowl wanted #2 ranked Georgia and Herschel Walker back again. So the SEC took the higher-ranked team – #2 Georgia over #3 Alabama.

___ **QUESTION 8:** LSU and Ole Miss.

___ **QUESTION 9:** He got heat stroke suffered at Picture Day and died early, which contributed to the effort to always keep UGA cool on game days – hence the air-conditioned dog house and bags of ice for UGA to lay on during sweltering game days in the Deep South.

___ **QUESTION 10:** George Haffner.

___ **QUESTION 11:** B – The Veer.

___ **QUESTION 12:** B – Fred Brown, 1960.

___ **QUESTION 13:** Garrison Hearst (1990-92) did it 16 times; Rodney Hampton (1987-89) is third with 12 100-yard games.

___ **QUESTION 14:** Lars Tate and Willie McClendon.

___ **QUESTION 15:** The Georgia Bulldogs and the Chicago Bears.

___ **QUESTION 16:** 80.

___ **QUESTION 17:** A –Ben Zambiasi, 1976 Cotton Bowl.

___ **QUESTION 18:** It was 72 yards, the longest attempt ever by Butler.

___ **QUESTION 19:** Bully.

___ **QUESTION 20:** True – 54.3%, 12-9-2.

___ **QUESTION 21:** September 30, 1995, by Alabama.

___ **QUESTION 22:** Hines Ward.

___ **QUESTION 23:** Georgia is 51-53-8.

___ **QUESTION 24:** 1938.

___ **QUESTION 25:** 104.

___ **QUESTION 26:** Kicker Brandon Coutu.

___ **QUESTION 27:** A – Charley Trippi.

___ **QUESTION 28:** Walker holds 68 records: 11 NCAA records, 16 SEC records, and 41 UGA records.

___ **QUESTION 29:** D – Billy Butler.

___ **QUESTION 30:** Jake Scott, who had ten of those in 1968 for 175 interception return yards.

___ **QUESTION 31:** Bulldogs' play-by-play man Ed Thilenius.

___ **QUESTION 32:** False. In 1977 the Dawgs gave up 191 points and scored just 157 in going 5-6.

___ **QUESTION 33:** It was 84 years earlier, in 1922. UGA is 18-2 against Vanderbilt on homecoming day.

___ **QUESTION 34:** Champ Bailey. For example, when UGA upset undefeated LSU in 1998 at Tiger Stadium, Bailey had 195 all-purpose yards, played 96 snaps on defense with two tackles, caught seven passes, scored a touchdown, and received on special teams.

___ **QUESTION 35:** D – Cotton.

___ **QUESTION 36:** Pat Dye was 7-5-0 against UGA while head coach at Auburn.

___ **QUESTION 37:** D – sixteen.

___ **QUESTION 38:** A – Kevin McLee.

___ **QUESTION 39:** False. Walker averaged 161 yards per game in SEC road games; 157 yards per game in SEC games at Sanford Stadium; and 216 yards per game against the Florida Gators in Jacksonville.

___ **QUESTION 40:** No. Vince Dooley was 8-10-2 in bowl games.

Got your Second Quarter total? ___ / 40
Good luck at Half Time!

Chapter Four

HALF TIME

QUESTION 1: Which Uga is the winningest Uga ever?

QUESTION 2: Name the opponent for each of these rivalry games:
- ➤ Clean, Old-Fashioned Hate
- ➤ Deep South's Oldest Rivalry
- ➤ The World's Largest Outdoor Cocktail Party

QUESTION 3: What was the record of the Georgia "Red and Black" at Herty Field?
- a) 20-20-0
- b) 31-7-2
- c) 18-20-2
- d) 24-14-2

QUESTION 4: What chant did Georgia fans once taunt the Gators with at the end of the game?
- a) Na-Na-Hey-Hey-Goodbye!
- b) Four Whole Days! Four Whole Days!
- c) GatorGator How'd you like to bite my @$$?
- d) None of the above. A Dawg would *never, ever* tease a Gator.

QUESTION 5: Of the major BCS bowl games (Orange, Sugar, Fiesta, Rose) which one have the Dawgs never played in?

QUESTION 6: What is the official name of US 80, running from Hopeulikit to Statesboro, GA?

QUESTION 7: What is the name of the creek that runs under Sanford Stadium?

QUESTION 8: The Georgia-Florida game was not played in 1943. Why?

QUESTION 9: When was the last time that Georgia was shut out by Auburn?

QUESTION 10: The Georgia-Auburn game has been played in five "neutral" sites. Name three.

QUESTION 11: Who was William Tate, after whom the Tate Student Center was named at UGA?

QUESTION 12: Riddle me this: Why do Tennessee fans like Orange so much?

QUESTION 13: The name of what famous running back adorns the traditional athletic residence hall at UGA?
   a) Bob McWhorter
   b) Herschel Walker
   c) Charley Trippi
   d) Spud Chandler

QUESTION 14: Who held the UGA record for sacks broken by Richard Tardits?

QUESTION 15: True or False: 1982 Heisman Trophy winner Herschel Walker's #34 has been retired in every sport at UGA.

QUESTION 16: The elongated G logo was crafted by a BFA graduate of UGA at the prompting of new Head

Coach Vince Dooley. For the curious, the Green Bay Packer elongated G preceded the UGA "G," which was cleared with NFL licensing at the time. The Packers abandoned that "G" but subsequently returned to it. The Dawgs have a 70% winning percentage since adopting the elongated G in 1964. Who designed it?

QUESTION 17: Georgia has won 52.0% of the games they've played that were televised on ESPN. As if related to the "Curse of Gameday," the Dawgs confront mediocrity on ESPN, where they are 25-23-1 through 2007. What was the first Georgia game on ESPN?

QUESTION 18: True or false: Georgia has an all-time winning record at Georgia Tech's Grant Field.

QUESTION 19: The largest margin of victory by Georgia on the gridiron is 108 points. Who was the victim?

QUESTION 20: How many All-American footballers has UGA had through the 2008 season?
   a) 44
   b) 67
   c) 32
   d) 88

QUESTION 21: UGA SID Dan Magill took a liking to the little white bullpup the Seiler's brought to the game on September 29, 1956, and suggested to Wally Butts that the Seiler's bring little Uga to subsequent games. An "Uga" has been present at every UGA football game since, with the exception of four games. On October 14, 1986, before the Vandy game, Uga IV jumped off a hotel room bed in Nashville and injured his knee. Who stood in?

QUESTION 22: "Mr. Bulldog," as you recall, was Herschel Scott of Monroe, and he attended more consecutive UGA games than any other fan. The streak started in 1962, and Scott died years later after a particularly bad loss to . . . which SEC opponent?

QUESTION 23: What movie did an Uga appear in?
   a) *Midnight in the Garden of Good and Evil*
   b) *Leatherheads*
   c) *Brother Where Art Thou*
   d) *The Blue Collar Comedy Tour Rides Again*

QUESTION 24: On November 12, 1994, before a national television audience on ESPN, Georgia and Auburn tied 13-13. The Glory goes to Georgia. This game is notable for two reasons. One is that Georgia broke Terry Bowden's string of 20 wins without a loss as coach at Auburn, knocking probation-status Auburn out of the national championship hunt. What's the other reason?

QUESTION 25: UGA offensive coordinator George Haffner called the play that led to Lindsey Scott's famous 93 yard dash to score in the 1980 Gator game. What was the name of the play?

QUESTION 26: When asked if he gets tired running all of those yards in a game, Herschel Walker responded, "Hey, the ball ain't heavy." On the other hand, how much does Walker's Heisman Trophy weigh?

QUESTION 27: The longest kickoff return ever by a Bulldog was by Lindsay Scott, who returned a 99 yard kickoff for a touchdown against LSU on October 14, 1978. Who tied that record, and when?

QUESTION 28: Who is the most-losing quarterback in the last half-century of Georgia football?

QUESTION 29: Bulldog offensive lineman Matt Stinchcomb was an All-American in 1997 and 1998. His brother, offensive lineman Jon Stinchcomb, was an All-American in 2002. What was their combined playing weight?
   a) 553 pounds
   b) 601 pounds
   c) 714 pounds
   d) 629 pounds

QUESTION 30: For his career linebacker Mo Lewis had 14 sacks. He got four of those in one game, against Ole Miss on October 14, 1989, and had a total of ten sacks in 1989. What type of pet did Mo keep at McWhorter Hall?

Chapter Four Answer Key

Time to find out how you did – put a check mark next to the questions you answered correctly, and when you are done be sure and add up your score. You'll need it after the final chapter to find out your Bulldogs IQ!

___ **QUESTION 1:** Uga VI was 98-30 (76.5%) with 20+ victories over ranked opponents.

___ **QUESTION 2:** Clean, Old-Fashioned Hate (Georgia Tech); Deep South's Oldest Rivalry (Auburn); and The World's Largest Outdoor Cocktail Party (Florida).

___ **QUESTION 3:** D – 24-14-2.

___ **QUESTION 4:** B – Four Whole Days! Four Whole Days!

___ **QUESTION 5:** Fiesta.

___ **QUESTION 6:** Erk Russell Memorial Highway.

___ **QUESTION 7:** Tanyard Creek.

___ **QUESTION 8:** Florida did not field a team.

___ **QUESTION 9:** 1963.

___ **QUESTION 10:** Atlanta, Macon, Montgomery, Savannah, or Columbus.

___ **QUESTION 11:** Dean of Men until 1980. He died the night of the Clemson game, on his birthday.

___ **QUESTION 12:** Because you can wear it to the game on Saturday, for hunting on Sunday, and to pick up trash on the side of the road on Monday (also works for Clemson).

___ **QUESTION 13:** A – Bob McWhorter.

___ **QUESTION 14:** Defensive tackle Jimmy Payne (1978-82).

___ **QUESTION 15:** True.

___ **QUESTION 16:** Anne Donaldson, wife of then-backfield coach Jim Donaldson.

___ **QUESTION 17:** Versus Auburn, November 17, 1984.

___ **QUESTION 18:** True – 53.2%, 24-20-3.

___ **QUESTION 19:** Alabama Presbyterian, October 4, 1913. Running back Bob McWhorter ran all day long.

___ **QUESTION 20:** B – 67.

___ **QUESTION 21:** Otto, brother of UGA IV was called in as a replacement, going 3-1-0 with only a loss to Florida.

___ **QUESTION 22:** "Mr. Bulldog's" final game was the 2003 loss to Tennessee.

___ **QUESTION 23:** A – *Midnight in the Garden of Good and Evil*.

___ **QUESTION 24:** This is the last tie in the series. Subsequently the NCAA adopted an overtime rule.

___ **QUESTION 25:** Left 76.

___ **QUESTION 26:** It weighs 25 pounds.

___ **QUESTION 27:** Thomas Brown tied Scott's mark in 2006 against Tennessee.

___ **QUESTION 28:** Larry Rakestraw, 1961-63, who was 10-16-4 but had a better passing efficiency than Fran Tarkenton.

___ **QUESTION 29:** D – 629 pounds.

___ **QUESTION 30:** A boa constrictor.

Got your Half Time total? ___ / 30
Good luck in the Third Quarter!

Chapter Five

THIRD QUARTER

QUESTION 1: Can you name the three quarterbacks who all started for Georgia in 2006?

QUESTION 2: Who ranks second, third and fourth on the UGA all-time career rushing list behind Herschel Walker?

QUESTION 3: Name three Bulldogs who have been overall #1 picks in the NFL draft.

QUESTION 4: On November 6, 1976, Florida Coach Doug Dickey sealed a reputation for lousy judgment in the third quarter of the 1976 Cocktail Party. With Florida leading 27-13 at the half, the Bulldogs came out fired up by James Brown and cut the Gator lead to a single touchdown. Then, facing fourth-and-one on his own 29, Dickey had RB Earl Carr go for the first down; he was stopped cold by Ronnie Swoopes, Jeff Sanders and the rest of the Junkyard Dawgs. Georgia took the ball back and that momentum shift carried the Bulldogs to victory, 41-27. What is the play forever known as?

QUESTION 5: What UGA player holds the school record for most offensive plays in a career?
   a) Herschel Walker
   b) Fran Tarkenton
   c) Champ Baileu
   d) David Greene

QUESTION 6: UGA is legendary for its kicking game. Who holds the record for most PAT's in a single game at UGA, with ten?
    a) Charlie Trippi
    b) Kevin Butler
    c) Kanon Parkman
    d) John Kasay

QUESTION 7: Did Vince Dooley and Steve Spurrier ever coach against each other in the Cocktail Party?

QUESTION 8: A Georgia Bulldog quarterback holds the SEC record for consecutive pass attempts without an interception, at 214. Who is it?
    a) Frank Tarkenton
    b) Eric Zeier
    c) David Greene
    d) Buck Belue

QUESTION 9: True or false: UGA has a winning record when Lee Corso and ESPN Gameday are in Athens.

QUESTION 10: The Dawgs are the only SEC football team to have played in three different Sugar Bowl venues. Only one other team has played Sugar Bowls in three different stadiums. Name the team.

QUESTION 11: True or False: Georgia has never won the Cotton Bowl?

QUESTION 12: True or false: Georgia Bulldog great Ray Goff won his last game at quarterback against the Gators and also won his first game as head coach against the Gators.

QUESTION **13:** John Heisman's winning percentage (71.1%) against the Red and Black from 1895 to 1916. Heisman was 13-5-2 against UGA.   Name the three schools that Coach Trophy coached against UGA.

QUESTION **14:** So we just told you that the University of Georgia has played in Sugar Bowls in three different stadiums. Now . . . can you name those venues?

QUESTION **15:** Georgia's top three freshman rushers of all time are Herschel Walker (1980) 1,616 yards; Knowshon Moreno (2007) 1,273 yards; and Rodney Hampton (1987) 890 yards. Name numbers four and five on the list.

QUESTION **16:** What was unique about the 2007 Bulldogs backfield when it came to freshman rushers?

QUESTION **17:** What do Matthew Stafford, Frank Sinkwich, and Johnny Rausch have in common, besides playing quarterback at UGA?

QUESTION **18:** A big day for a back is to rush for 200 yards. Seven Dawgs have done it a total of fifteen times. How many belong to Herschel Walker?

QUESTION **19:** Who rushed for more yards as a freshman in the Georgia-Florida game, Herschel Walker (1980) or Knowshon Moreno (2007)?

QUESTION **20:** On October 14, 1978, Georgia went to LSU and took on the #6, undefeated Tigers. Before the game, UGA III confronted LSU's mighty mascot, Mike the Tiger, and barked the big cat into cowering submission. Coach

Dooley saw the confrontation, and rushed back into the locker rooms and said to his team, "Let's go, men . . . we've got 'em tonight!" What was the result of the game:

    a) The Tigers beat the Dawgs 24-17

    b) The Dawgs beat the Tigers 24-17

    c) It was a tie

QUESTION 21: Which Bulldog was SEC Player of the Year in 1992?

QUESTION 22: Who held the UGA record for career rushing before Herschel Walker?

    a) Kevin McLee

    b) Frank Sinkwich

    c) Willie McClendon

QUESTION 23: Which Uga was on the sideline for the national championship in 1980?

QUESTION 24: Georgia played a total of 17 games against teams coached by Paul "Bear" Bryant. Bryant coached three teams against UGA – Alabama, Kentucky, and Texas A&M. What is the Bulldogs' record against the Bear?

    a) 12-4-1

    b) 7-9-1

    c) 5-12-0

    d) 7-7-3

QUESTION 25: Name the first three UGA teams to win 11 games or more.

QUESTION 26: Since 1947, the Bulldogs have gone to nine Sugar Bowls and gone 4-5-0 in those games. Three different Georgia players have been named Sugar Bowl MVP. Who are they?

QUESTION 27: The following Supreme Court cases all share one thing in common: Curtis Publishing Co. v. Butts, 388 U.S. 130 (1967); Allen v. The Regents of the University of Georgia (304 US 439); and NCAA v. Board of Regents of the University of Oklahoma 468 U.S. 85 (1984). What is the common theme?

QUESTION 28: QB Zeke Bratkowski completed 360 of 734 pass attempts from 1952-53, and was a three-time All-SEC ('51, '52, '53) selection and twice an All-American ('52, '53). He also enjoyed a long career in the NFL, playing 14 years in the pros, and earning two Super Bowl rings with the Green Bay Packers. True or false: Bratkowski is the most distinguished UGA quarterback to never play in a bowl game.

QUESTION 29: When Herschel Walker was in high school, he ran the hundred in 9.5 seconds and his team won the class-A high school championship in Georgia. Name one of three other sports where Herschel was a state champ.

QUESTION 30: In 1912, the University of Georgia defeated the University of Alabama 13-9 at Driving Park in Columbus. Georgia Coach W. A. Cunningham had Hooks Autrey dress in his civilian travel clothes. On UGA's first possession, he then sent ten men onto the field, and had Autrey line up casually, just in bounds of the field. Autrey sprinted down field with the snap, caught the ball, and downed himself at the ten. A fight broke out on the field. Subsequently, a specific college football rule change required all players to play in specified uniforms. Why else is this game significant?

QUESTION 31: In addition to Georgia, three other teams were designated "National Champions" for 1927 by the nine organizations authorized to do so. What were the other three teams?

QUESTION 32: Terry Hoage set an SEC record for interceptions in a season, with 12. What season did he do it?
   a) 1980
   b) 1981
   c) 1982
   d) 1983

QUESTION 33: What Bulldog kicker holds the NCAA record for career field goals made?
   a) Kanon Parkman
   b) Billy Bennett
   c) Kevin Butler

QUESTION 34: The 1946 Georgia Bulldogs were undefeated, won 11 games, won the Sugar Bowl, and were placed third in the AP poll at the end of the season. The teams they ranked behind, Army and Notre Dame, were both 9-0-1. Why Did UGA rank behind two teams with fewer wins and a tie each?

QUESTION 35: How many field goals did legendary UGA kicker Kevin Butler make in his career from 1981-84?

QUESTION 36: Of Florida, Georgia Tech, Tennessee, and Auburn, against which teams did Ray Goff have a winning record as head coach?

QUESTION 37: How many Heisman Trophy winners have played in the Georgia-Auburn game over the years?

QUESTION 38: On November 18, 1959, Wally Butts sent Francis Tarkenton on the field against the Auburn Tigers, coached by his friend and former assistant Shug Jordan. The Dawgs, losers of six straight to Auburn, trailed 13-7 when Tarkenton drove the Dawgs down field and hit Bill Herron for a touchdown with 25 seconds on the clock. Then Auburn fumbled on its own 45 and a UGA guard recovered the ball to preserve the win. Name the guard who sealed the game by recovering that fumble.

QUESTION 39: True or false: Georgia has a winning record in the 16 games the Dawgs have played at Death Valley, Clemson, South Carolina.

QUESTION 40: Herschel Walker averaged 5.29 yards per rush as a Bulldog in 1980, which is a UGA record. Whose record did Herschel break?
   a) Ray Goff, 5.25 ypr
   b) Charley Trippi, 5.27 ypr
   c) Frank Sinkwich, 5.28 ypr

Chapter Five Answer Key

Time to find out how you did – put a check mark next to the questions you answered correctly, and when you are done be sure and add up your score. You'll need it after the final chapter to find out your Bulldogs IQ!

___ **QUESTION 1:** Matt Stafford, Joe Cox, and Joe Tereshinski III.

___ **QUESTION 2:** Garrison Hearst, Lars Tate and Knowshon Moreno respectively.

___ **QUESTION 3:** Charlie Trippi (1947); Harry Babcock (1953); and Matthew Stafford (2009).

___ **QUESTION 4:** Dickey's call is forever immortalized as "Fourth And Dumb."

___ **QUESTION 5:** D – David Greene.

___ **QUESTION 6:** C – Kanon Parkman in 1994 versus Northeastern Louisiana (tied George Jernigan's number versus Furman a half-century before).

___ **QUESTION 7:** Yes and no. Spurrier was never head coach versus Dooley, but he was Florida's quarterbacks coach in 1978 when the Wonderdogs beat Florida 24-22.

___ **QUESTION 8:** C – David Greene.

___ **QUESTION 9:** False – the Dawgs are 3-7-0 with Gameday in town.

___ **QUESTION 10:** West Virginia, the Dawgs opponent in Atlanta in 2006.

___ **QUESTION 11:** False – UGA is 2-1-0 in the Cotton Bowl game.

___ **QUESTION 12:** True.

___ **QUESTION 13:** Auburn, Clemson, and Georgia Tech.

___ **QUESTION 14:** Tulane Stadium, the New Orleans Superdome, and the Georgia Dome in Atlanta.

___ **QUESTION 15:** Thomas Brown (2004) 875 yards and Keith Henderson (1985) 731 yards.

___ **QUESTION 16:** Three of the top ten freshman rushers ever at UGA were on the roster at the same time: Knowshon Moreno (2007, 2nd), Thomas Brown (2004, 4th), and Kregg Lumpkin (2003, 9th).

___ **QUESTION 17:** All three were drafted in the first round by the Detroit Lions.

___ **QUESTION 18:** *Nine* of those games.

___ **QUESTION 19:** Walker, with 238 yards.

___ **QUESTION 20:** B – the Dawgs beat the Tigers 24-17.

___ **QUESTION 21:** Garrison Hearst, who also won the Doak Walker Award as the top running back in the NCAA.

___ **QUESTION 22:** A – Kevin McLee, who rushed for 2,581 yards from 1975-77.

___ **QUESTION 23:** Uga III (AKA Seiler's Uga Three).

___ **QUESTION 24:** C, 5-12-0.

___ **QUESTION 25:** 1946 (11-0); 1971 (11-1); and 1980 (12-0).

___ **QUESTION 26:** Tailbacks Herschel Walker (1981) and Musa Smith (2003) and defensive end Marcus Howard (2008).

___ **QUESTION 27:** They are all cases that involve Georgia football.

___ **QUESTION 28:** True. Bratkowski's Dawgs went 15-17-0 in his three years at quarterback and never received a bowl bid.

___ **QUESTION 29:** He won the 100 meters, the 220 meters, and the shot put.

___ **QUESTION 30:** It was the first football game ever played in Columbus.

___ **QUESTION 31:** Illinois, Notre Dame, and Yale.

___ **QUESTION 32:** C – 1982.

___ **QUESTION 33:** B – Billy Bennett.

___ **QUESTION 34:** Because Army and Notre Dame tied each other, 0-0.

___ **QUESTION 35:** He made 77.

___ **QUESTION 36:** Only Tech (5-2). Ray was 0-5 versus Tennessee, 1-6 versus Florida, and 2-4-1 versus Auburn.

___ **QUESTION 37:** Surprisingly, just four: Frank Sinkwich (UGA), Pat Sullivan (Auburn), Herschel Walker (UGA), and Bo Jackson (Auburn).

___ **QUESTION 38:** Pat Dye, later to be Auburn's coach, was the All-American UGA guard who fell on the fumble.

___ **QUESTION 39:** True – UGA is 8-6-2 (56.3% winning percentage) at Death Valley.

___ **QUESTION 40:** C – Frank Sinkwich, 5.28 ypr.

Got your Third Quarter total? __ / 40
Good luck at Half Time!

Chapter Six

FOURTH QUARTER

QUESTION 1: How many football games did Georgia win before Vince Dooley became head coach in 1964?

QUESTION 2: Herschel Walker holds the UGA and Sanford Stadium record for yards rushing in a single game, set in 1980. How many yards did he gain? And who was the opponent?

QUESTION 3: Who has the record for most rushing yards by a Bulldog against the Gators, at 239 total yards rushing?
    a) Herschel Walker
    b) Charley Trippi
    c) Knowshon Moreno
    d) Frank Sinkwich

QUESTION 4: From 1920 to 1948 the Georgia-Auburn (The Deep South's Oldest Rivalry) game was played in Columbus, Georgia – a total of 39 meetings. How many of those games were won by UGA?
    a) 11
    b) 14
    c) 21
    d) 27

QUESTION 5: A Georgia kicker, once upon a time, went to two Sugar Bowls, upset top-ranked Clemson with four field goals, and became the source of rare Heisman speculation for a kicker. Who was he?

QUESTION 6: The most points ever scored by a Bulldog in a single game is 30. Who did it, and when?

QUESTION 7: The most touchdowns scored by a Bulldog on the Gators is four. Who did it?
   a) Charlie Trippi
   b) Robert Edwards
   c) Herschel Walker
   d) Knowshon Moreno

QUESTION 8: The 2005 Georgia-Auburn game, played in Athens, had more lead changes than any non-overtime UGA-Auburn game, and half came in the fourth quarter. How many total lead changes were there?

QUESTION 9: In 1953, Georgia lost to Auburn 39-18 as Shug Jordan alternated "running" and "passing" platoons in what he termed the "X/Y Offense." The quarterback for the "running" squad still went six-for-nine with 116 yards passing. Who was he?

QUESTION 10: The 1985 Georgia Bulldogs beat Clemson 20-13. What Bulldog determined the outcome of the game with two fourth-quarter interceptions on defense?

QUESTION 11: The Georgia-Georgia Tech game has been played either 100 or 102 times since 1893. The Bulldogs record against Tech is either 59-38-5 or 59-36-5. Why is there a dispute about the number of Tech wins?

QUESTION 12: The return record before Lindsay Scott was owned by four Bulldogs. Buster Mott, against NYU, 1931; Lamar Davis against Tulane, 1940; Jimmy

Campagna against Auburn, 1952; and Gene Washington, against Clemson, 1973. What is unique about Washington's return?

QUESTION 13: How many rushes did Herschel Walker have in his career?

QUESTION 14: One Bulldog head coach is undefeated in bowl game play, winning every bowl game he coached with the Red and Black. Who is the undefeated post-season Bulldog coach?
   a) Jim Donnan
   b) Ray Goff
   c) Mark Richt
   d) Wally Butts

QUESTION 15: On November 7, 1942, UGA went into the Florida game and beat the Gators 75-0, which is the worst shutout UGA has ever handed an SEC opponent. What else is significant about this game, where eventual Heisman winner Frank Sinkwich led the Dawgs?

QUESTION 16: Charlie Britt's 100-yard interception return for a touchdown vs. Florida in 1959, which sealed a 21-10 victory for the Dawgs, is the longest on record in the Georgia-Florida rivalry. Who tipped the pass before it was intercepted?

QUESTION 17: In Georgia's four-overtime, nine-come-from-behind, 56-49 victory over Auburn on November 19, 1996, quarterback Brian Smith was relieved by Mike Bobo with the Dawgs trailing 28-7. How many yards did Bobo pass for in the epic comeback win?

QUESTION 18: The first Georgia-Florida game played in Jacksonville was on November 7, 1915, when Coach W. A. Cunningham led his Red and Black against the Florida eleven. Who won?

QUESTION 19: Four Tereshinskis, including three named Joe, have suited up for the Red and Black. Joe Sr. played tight end after World War II. Joe T was a center in the 1970s, and his brother Wally was a tight end. Joe III was a quarterback in the 2000s. How many of the Tereshinskis played for SEC champion teams?

QUESTION 20: UGA has been shut out 127 times. Plus, they also shut out the opposition on 21 of those occasions. When was the last scoreless tie involving the Dawgs?

QUESTION 21: In 2001, on the road in Knoxville, Tennessee, David Greene completed a TD pass to Verron Haynes with five seconds on the clock to upend the Vols 26-24. What was legendary play-by-play man Larry Munson's reaction?

QUESTION 22: UGA IV had a 73.1% winning percentage and was the winningest UGA up to that time. He succeeded his father in 1981, and stayed on the sidelines through the end of the Dooley era and into Ray Goff's first year as head coach. UGA IV went to bowl games every year. What was the record of UGA with UGA IV on the postseason sideline?

QUESTION 23: The 1937 Bulldogs were captained by All-American fullback Bill Hartman. Bill Hartman was the tenth Georgia Bulldog and the fourth Georgia backfield player to be named All-American. He was later an assistant coach for the Dawgs for 17 seasons. What did he coach?

   a) Special teams
   b) Backfield
   c) Defensive line
   d) Strength and conditioning

QUESTION 24: True or false: The last UGA head coach to have a losing record at home was Ray Goff.

QUESTION 25: Mark Richt-coached Bulldog teams have a 70% winning percentage at night – the Dawgs are 15-7 after dark through 2008. Are the Dawgs better at night at home or on the road?

QUESTION 26: UGA's Cow Nalley made the final score to win the 1894 Auburn game, 10-8. He died in 1902, in Atlanta, with a smile on his face. Why?

QUESTION 27: On November 16, 1996, Uga V roamed the sidelines at Jordan-Hare stadium during the four-overtime, 56-49 win. Early in the game he lunged at the groin of an Auburn receiver, Robert Baker. What nickname did Uga receive thereafter?

QUESTION 28: A Georgia team holds the record for largest deficit ever overcome (25 points) to win a New Year's Day bowl game. What game, and what opponent?

QUESTION 29: December 2, 1978, Buck Belue takes to the field with 1:52 on the clock trailing Tech by seven. Belue drives the Dawgs 84 yards down field, connecting on a 42 yard, fourth down TD pass to flanker Amp

Arnold. The Dawgs win the game on a two-point conversion run by Arnold to pull out a 29-28 win for the "Wonder Dogs." How many come from behind wins did the "Wonder Dogs" have in 1978?

QUESTION 30: For his career, Vince Dooley won against Florida based on crunch-time play by his defense and exceptional execution in the fourth quarter by the Dawgs' offense. He was 17-7-1 all-time versus the Gators and won seven of his last nine. What particular circumstance occurred in his first coaching win over the Gators, in 1964?

QUESTION 31: How much time was left on the clock of the 1981 Sugar Bowl when All-American Scott Woerner picked off freshman Irish QB Blair Kiel to seal the Dawgs' national title win over Notre Dame?

QUESTION 32: Since the beginning of football time, UGA and Alabama have played 22 games decided by just one score. True or false: Georgia has a losing record against Alabama in games decided by one score.

QUESTION 33: There is a consensus that ringing the bell started after a game in 1901; the freshmen were made to ring the bell until midnight. What was the game and the result?

QUESTION 34: In Ray Goff's debut as head coach of the Georgia Bulldogs in 1989, UGA won the opener at Sanford Stadium, versus Baylor. Coach Goff observed to Larry Munson after the game "the kicking game was good today, because you have to have good kicking for the kicking to be good." I wrote it down. Why did he say this?

QUESTION 35: Wally Butts had a 71.7% winning percentage at Sanford Stadium. From 1939 to 1960, Butts was 64-24-4 at home and his longest home winning streak was 12 games. It started with a November 30, 1940 win over Georgia Tech (21-19). Who broke the streak?

QUESTION 36: UGA had 691 points in the final AP Poll of the 1981 season. Georgia started the season at #11, and, despite a loss to Clemson in the third game of the season, clawed its way back to #2 in the final regular season AP Poll and went back to the Sugar Bowl and played Pitt. Who finished ahead of UGA in the regular season poll and won the national title?

QUESTION 37: NFL Draft Match Game, Part I:

1943: Frank Sinkwich	Chicago Cardinals
1947: Charley Trippi	Detroit Lions
1948: Dan Edwards	Detroit Lions
1949: Johnny Rauch	Miami Dolphins
1953: Harry Babcock	New Orleans Saints
1969: Bill Stanfill	Pittsburgh Steelers
1972: Royce Smith	San Francisco 49ers

QUESTION 38: NFL Draft Match Game, Part II:

1982: Lindsay Scott	Arizona Cardinals
1989: Tim Worley	New England Patriots
1990: Ben Smith	New Orleans Saints
1990: Rodney Hampton	New York Giants
1993: Garrison Hearst	Oakland Raiders
1994: Bernard Williams	Philadelphia Eagles

1998: Robert Edwards   Philadelphia Eagles
1999: Champ Bailey   Pittsburgh Steelers
1999: Matt Stinchcomb   Washington Redskins

QUESTION 39: NFL Draft Match Game, Part III:
2001: Richard Seymour   Carolina Panthers
2001: Marcus Stroud   Cincinnati Bengals
2002: Charles Grant   Denver Broncos
2003: Johnathan Sullivan Denver Broncos
2003: George Foster   Detroit Lions
2004: Ben Watson   Jacksonville Jaguars
2005: Thomas Davis   New England Patriots
2005: David Pollack   New England Patriots
2009: Matthew Stafford   New Orleans Saints
2009: Knowshon Moreno   New Orleans Saints

QUESTION 40: What is greater, the number of coaching ties by Vince Dooley or the number of wins by his predecessor, Johnny Griffith?

Chapter Six Answer Key

Time to find out how you did – put a check mark next to the questions you answered correctly, and when you are done be sure and add up your score. You'll need it after the final chapter to find out your Bulldogs IQ!

___ **QUESTION 1:** 351, against 228 losses.

___ **QUESTION 2:** 283 yards, versus Vanderbilt.

___ **QUESTION 3:** B – Charley Trippi.

___ **QUESTION 4:** C – 21 (UGA was 21-16-2 in the series in Columbus).

___ **QUESTION 5:** Kevin Butler. From 1981-84, the Bulldogs went 38-8-2 behind his foot.

___ **QUESTION 6:** RB Robert Edwards scored five touchdowns against South Carolina on September 3, 1994. He scored four rushing, including one for 58 yards, and one receiving, good for 45 yards.

___ **QUESTION 7:** B – Robert Edwards.

___ **QUESTION 8:** Eight, as Auburn upset Georgia at home.

___ **QUESTION 9:** Vince Dooley.

___ **QUESTION 10:** Rover back John Little.

___ **QUESTION 11:** The disputed games arise from the 1943 and 1944 games. Georgia refuses to recognize the two games because Tech used military personnel in the games.

___ **QUESTION 12:** It is the only one that took place at home, and is still the longest kickoff return for touchdown ever at Sanford Stadium. Mott's was at Yankee Stadium; Davis's was at Tulane Stadium; Campagna's was in Columbus.

___ **QUESTION 13:** 994.

___ **QUESTION 14:** A – Jim Donnan.

___ **QUESTION 15:** It was the first week UGA had ever been ranked #1 by the AP.

___ **QUESTION 16:** Dawgs' guard Pat Dye, who would later coach at Auburn.

___ **QUESTION 17:** 360 yards.

___ **QUESTION 18:** Georgia, 39-0.

___ **QUESTION 19:** All of them (1942, 1946, 1976, 2005).

___ **QUESTION 20:** October 30, 1954, in Birmingham against the Alabama Crimson Tide.

___ **QUESTION 21:** "We just stepped on their face with a hob-nailed boot and broke their nose! We just crushed their face!"

___ **QUESTION 22:** It was 4-3-2.

___ **QUESTION 23:** B – Backfield.

___ **QUESTION 24:** False. Ray Goff's winning percentage was 69.0% at home. The last coach with a losing home record was Johnny Griffith (1961-63).

___ **QUESTION 25:** On the road. Richt's teams are 8-0 at night on the road, but 7-7 at night at home.

___ **QUESTION 26:** The last thing he heard on this Earth was that Georgia had just defeated Auburn 27-5.

___ **QUESTION 27:** "The Dawg who defended his turf."

___ **QUESTION 28:** It was the 2000 Outback Bowl, against Purdue.

___ **QUESTION 29:** Five.

___ **QUESTION 30:** Kicker Bobby Etter botched a field goal and it became a touchdown.

___ **QUESTION 31:** Just 2:56 left on the clock.

___ **QUESTION 32:** False – Georgia's winning percentage versus Alabama in games decided by a touchdown or less is 10-8-4 (54.5%).

___ **QUESTION 33:** UGA and Auburn played to a scoreless tie in Atlanta.

___ QUESTION 34: The final score was 15-3, with all the scoring coming on field goals.

___ QUESTION 35: Wake Forest. The Demon Deacons beat UGA at home 14-7 on September 29, 1944.

___ QUESTION 36: Clemson.

___ QUESTION 37: NFL Draft Match Game, Part I Key:
1943: Frank Sinkwich (Detroit Lions)
1947: Charley Trippi (Chicago Cardinals)
1948: Dan Edwards (Pittsburgh Steelers)
1949: Johnny Rauch Detroit Lions)
1953: Harry Babcock (San Francisco 49ers)
1969: Bill Stanfill (Miami Dolphins)
1972: Royce Smith (New Orleans Saints)

___ QUESTION 38: NFL Draft Match Game, Part II Key:
1982: Lindsay Scott (New Orleans Saints)
1989: Tim Worley (Pittsburgh Steelers)
1990: Ben Smith (Philadelphia Eagles)
1990: Rodney Hampton New York Giants)
1993: Garrison Hearst (Arizona Cardinals)
1994: Bernard Williams (Philadelphia Eagles)
1998: Robert Edwards (New England Patriots)
1999: Champ Bailey Washington Redskins)
1999: Matt Stinchcomb (Oakland Raiders)

___ QUESTION 39: NFL Draft Match Game, Part III Key:
2001: Richard Seymour (New England Patriots)
2001: Marcus Stroud (Jacksonville Jaguars)
2002: Charles Grant (New Orleans Saints)
2003: Johnathan Sullivan (New Orleans Saints)
2003: George Foster (Denver Broncos)

2004: Ben Watson (New England Patriots)
2005: Thomas Davis (Carolina Panthers)
2005: David Pollack (Cincinnati Bengals)
2009: Matthew Stafford (Detroit Lions)
2009: Knowshon Moreno (Denver Broncos)

___ **QUESTION 40:** Neither. Dooley had 10 ties and Griffith had 10 wins as UGA head coach.

Got your Fourth Quarter total? ___ / 40
Good luck making it through Meaner than a Junkyard Dawg – not like we saved the toughest questions for last or anything!

Chapter Seven

MEANER THAN A JUNKYARD DAWG

QUESTION 1: In 1976 UGA (10-2) won the SEC and went to the Sugar Bowl behind the quarterback leadership of Ray Goff, who was running the veer offense. What was the nickname of the defense? And how many points did it give up per game?

QUESTION 2: Who recorded "Dooley's Junkyard Dogs" in 1975 and then performed it at the 50- yard line of Gator Bowl Stadium, decked out in bright red?

QUESTION 3: Can you name the front four of the 1975 "Junkyard Dawgs?"

QUESTION 4: The Junkyard Dogs were Erk Russell's innovative, cast-off defensive unit that dominated opponents in the mid-1970s using the Junkyard Eight line. The original 1975 Junkyard Dogs weighed just 208 pounds across the board. How many points per game did they give up?

QUESTION 5: On September 9, 2006, the Junkyard Dawgs reemerged to hang an 18-0 shutout on the South Carolina Gamecocks. Why is this significant?

QUESTION 6: Leonard Postosties of Jefferson, Georgia, prognosticated college football's losers for the coming game day, and at the height of his popularity was heard on 1,400 stations around the country plus on Armed Forces Radio. Leonard is, to our knowledge, the man who popularized the phrase "Red Clay Hounds of Georgia" (sorry Keith Jackson). He died on July 20, 2001, after decades on the air picking winners and losers, though the franchise endured for some time beyond. What was Leonard's real name? And when did he sign on the air? And what was his signature sign off line?

QUESTION 7: The 1975 Georgia Bulldogs are largely remembered for the Junkyard Dawg defense. The "Junkyard Eight" formation, built out of necessity, helped propel LB Ben Zambiasi and DB Bill Krug to All-SEC honors in 1975. But Georgia's premier All-American was its offensive captain. Who was he?
   a) Willie McClendon
   b) Kevin McLee
   c) Glynn Harrison
   d) Randy Johnson

QUESTION 8: Match Game: Match the Coach with his winning percentage at Sanford Stadium:
___ Harry Mehre	a. (.875)
___ Joel Hunt	b. (.830)
___ Wallace Butts	c. (.809)
___ Johnny Griffith	d. (.750)
___ Vince Dooley	e. (.733)
___ Ray Goff	f. (.720)
___ Jim Donnan	g. (.690)
___ Mark Richt	h. (.385)

QUESTION 9: Until 1920, the Georgia eleven were referred to as the "Red and Black." Then, in 1920, UGA went 8-0-1 under first-year coach and eventual legend Herman Stegeman. That November an Atlanta

sportswriter rechristened the Red and Black "the Bulldogs." Name the sportswriter.

QUESTION 10: Georgia has an 80.2% winning percentage on Homecoming Day. The Dawgs started playing Homecoming games on November 18, 1922, when they lost to Vandy 12-0. Georgia won every homecoming game until 1936, and is 68-16-2 overall on Homecoming. What team does Georgia least want to see for homecoming?

QUESTION 11: Larry Munson called 343 Georgia victories in his 42-season career. Who did he replace behind the mic for the Georgia games?

QUESTION 12: The best-known high school football program in Georgia is probably Valdosta High. Valdosta has 23 state football championships since the construction of its home field, Cleveland Field, in 1922. Valdosta also has six national prep titles. True or False: Valdosta High's Buck Belue won a national prep title before he won a National football title at UGA in 1980.

QUESTION 13: How many times have the Dawgs finished in the AP Top 20?

QUESTION 14: How far is the drive from Sanford Stadium in Athens to the Gator Bowl in Jacksonville, site of the Georgia-Florida "World's Largest Outdoor Cocktail Party"?

QUESTION 15: What is the name of the award given to the player who shows the most desire during spring drills at UGA?

QUESTION 16: On September 19, 1964, Lewis Grizzard covered his first Georgia game as a journalist – freshman Grizzard was hired by WAGA's Ed Thilenius to act as spotter on the opposing team, which as you may recall, was Alabama (it was also Vince Dooley's first game as head coach at UGA). How much money was Grizzard paid to act as spotter that day?

QUESTION 17: On March 23, 1982, Vince Dooley hired Hornsby Howell onto the football coaching staff. Howell, previously a coach at North Carolina A & T, joined Dooley's staff to run the scout team. What is Howell's place in UGA history?

QUESTION 18: In 1971, Vince Dooley successfully integrated the football team at the University of Georgia. How many of the five African-Americans who Dooley successfully recruited to UGA that season can you name?

QUESTION 19: The year Georgia was consensus national champion (1980), what was its preseason ranking by the Associated Press? When did Georgia move into the #1 slot?

QUESTION 20: Georgia fans generally acknowledge one national title, the consensus 1980 champions. But according to the NCAA, the Dawgs claim all or part of five national championships. Name any four of the eight organizations recognized by the NCAA that have conferred "official" National titles (other than 1980) on the Dawgs. Double points for naming the years, too.

QUESTION 21: The Georgia Bulldogs were a controversial National title choice after the 1980 season. The Dawgs were not highly ranked entering the season, and were expected to lose to Notre Dame in the Sugar Bowl (they won 13-7). Four-and-a-half #1 votes on the final AP ballot were not cast for the Dawgs. Who received those votes instead of undefeated Georgia?

QUESTION 22: Besides Herschel Walker, three other Bulldogs have had a number retired. Who are they (double credit – name the numbers):

QUESTION 23: UGA athletic director Damon Evans played wide receiver for Vince Dooley and Ray Goff, and when he was 34 became the AD at UGA and the first black AD in SEC history. What record did he set at Gainesville High School?

QUESTION 24: The longest touchdown run by a Bulldog is 105 yards by Frank McCutcheon, in a play against Tech on October 22, 1898. How is that possible?

QUESTION 25: Of the 259 televised games played by UGA through the start of last season (2008), how many have been decided by a single score?
- a) 22
- b) 43
- c) 66
- d) 93

QUESTION 26: UGA has played a total of 66 games on ABC television, many of them called by the legendary Keith "Red Clay Hounds of Georgia" Jackson. Do the

Bulldogs have a winning record before the cameras of ABC?

QUESTION 27: On November 19, 1996, Georgia and Auburn played one of the greatest football games of all time, a 56-49 win by the Dawgs in four overtimes. It was the 100th meeting between Auburn and UGA.   Led by the combination of Mike Bobo and Hines Ward, how many come-from-behind points were scored by the Bulldogs?

QUESTION 28: Georgia has played a total of nine Sugar Bowls, going 4-5-0.   Can you add the Sugar Bowl opponent for each game?

Date	Opponent	Score
1947	_____	20-10
1969	_____	2-16
1977	_____	3-27
1981	_____	17-10
1982	_____	20-24
1983	_____	23-27
2003	_____	26-13
2006	_____	35-38
2008	_____	41-10

QUESTION 29: Larry Munson Match Game:
Larry Munson retired as the play-by-play man on the Bulldogs broadcasts at the end of the 2007 season – the Sugar Bowl was his last call. For three generations of Georgia fans, it'll be hard to imagine another Voice.

Now, can you match the great Larry Munson calls to the games they came from? Your choices:
   a) 1973 Kentucky Game
   b) 1975 Florida Game
   c) 1980 Florida Game
   d) 1980 Tennessee Game
   e) 1982 Auburn Game
   f) 1984 Clemson Game
   g) 2002 Tennessee Game

   ➢ "He drove right over orange shirts just driving and running with those big thighs."
   ➢ "I broke my chair. I came right through a chair. A metal steel chair with about a five-inch cushion. I broke it. The booth came apart. The stadium . . . Well the stadium fell down."
   ➢ "Look at the Sugar falling out of the sky!"
   ➢ "Rex Robinson put them ahead, 17-16. The bench is unconscious."
   ➢ "So we'll try and kick one 100,000 miles, we hold it on our own forty-nine-and-a-half, sixty yards plus a foot and Butler kicks a long one, Butler kicks a long one, Oh my God! Oh My God! Oh my God! The stadium is worse than bonkers. Eleven seconds left and I can't believe what I saw. This is ungodly!"
   ➢ "Washington, thinking of Montreal and the Olympics ran out of his shoes!"
   ➢ "We just stepped on their face with a hobnailed boot and broke their nose. We just crushed their faces!"

QUESTION 30: Erk Russell describes the Junkyard Eight defense: "A Junkyard Dog is a dog completely dedicated to his task, that of defending his goal line. Further, he is very often a reject (from the offense) or the runt of the litter. Nobody wants him, and he is hungry. We had three walk-ons, four QBs, and three running backs in our original Junkyard Dog starting cast . . . a Junkyard Dog is one who must stretch and strain all of his potential just to survive. Then he can think about being good." Erk served as defensive coordinator for 192 games at UGA from 1964 through the 1981 Sugar Bowl. He created the Junkyard Eight defense and his teams held opponents to 17 or fewer points in 70% of games. What did Erk do to players after exceptional plays?

Chapter Seven Answer Key

Time to find out how you did – put a check mark next to the questions you answered correctly, and when you are done be sure and add up your score. You'll need it to find out your Bulldogs IQ!

___ **QUESTION 1:** The Junkyard Dogs; 12.1 ppg.

___ **QUESTION 2:** Augusta's Godfather of Soul, James Brown.

___ **QUESTION 3:** Lawrence Craft (LE), Brad Thompson (LT), Ronnie Swoopes (RT), and Dickey Clark (RE).

___ **QUESTION 4:** It was 16.4.

___ **QUESTION 5:** It was the first shutout of a Steve Spurrier-coached team since the Duke Blue Devils lost to Rutgers in 1987.

___ **QUESTION 6:** Leonard Postero. 1958. "Get me out of here Percy!"

___ **QUESTION 7:** D – Randy Johnson.

___ **QUESTION 8:** Harry Mehre (d), Joel Hunt (a), Wallace Butts (f), Johnny Griffith (h), Vince Dooley (c), Ray Goff (g), Jim Donnan (e), Mark Richt (b).

___ **QUESTION 9:** This is a bone of contention. Either Morgan Blake of the *Atlanta Journal* or the *Atlanta*

Constitution's Cliff Wheatley renamed UGA's gridiron team.

___ QUESTION 10: Alabama. The Crimson Tide won Georgia homecomings in 1947, 1949, 1951, 1953, and 1957.

___ QUESTION 11: Ed Thilenius.

___ QUESTION 12: False. Parade All-American Buck Belue (VHS, 1977) had to go to UGA to find his championship.

___ QUESTION 13: 29 times.

___ QUESTION 14: 342 miles.

___ QUESTION 15: The Coffee County Hustle Award.

___ QUESTION 16: $10.

___ QUESTION 17: Howell was the first African-American assistant coach on the football staff at UGA.

___ QUESTION 18: Horace King, Ed Appleby, Larry West, Clarence Pope and Chuck Kinnebrew.

___ QUESTION 19: #16. Georgia moved into the #1 slot after defeating Florida.

___ QUESTION 20: Berryman (1942); Board System (1927); DeVold (1942); Houlgate System (1942); Litkenhous (1942, 1968); Massey Ratings (1966); Poling System (1927, 1942); Williamson System (1942, 1946).

___ **QUESTION 21:** One-loss Pitt got 3.5 votes, and two-loss Florida State got one vote.

___ **QUESTION 22:** Charley Trippi (#61); Theron Sapp (#40); and Frank Sinkwich (#21).

___ **QUESTION 23:** Receptions, with 44 as a senior in 1987.

___ **QUESTION 24:** Back then the playing field was 110 yards long.

___ **QUESTION 25:** D – 93.

___ **QUESTION 26:** Yes. The Georgia Bulldogs have a 62.1% winning percentage on ABC television (40-24-2).

___ **QUESTION 27:** It was 49.

___ **QUESTION 28:** 1947 – North Carolina; 1969 – Arkansas; 1977, 1982 – Pitt; 1981 – Notre Dame; 1983 – Penn State; 2003 – Florida State; 2006 – West Virginia; 2008 – Hawaii.

___ **QUESTION 29:** Larry Munson Match Game:
  - ➢ "He drove right over orange shirts just driving and running with those big thighs." (1980 Tennessee Game)
  - ➢ "I broke my chair. I came right through a chair. A metal steel chair with about a five-inch cushion. I broke it. The booth came apart. The stadium . . . Well the stadium fell down." (1980 Florida Game)

- "Look at the Sugar falling out of the sky!" (1982 Auburn Game)
- "Rex Robinson put them ahead, 17-16. The bench is unconscious." (1973 Kentucky Game)
- "So we'll try and kick one 100,000 miles, we hold it on our own forty-nine-and-a-half, sixty yards plus a foot and Butler kicks a long one, Butler kicks a long one, Oh my God! Oh My God! Oh my God! The stadium is worse than bonkers. Eleven seconds left and I can't believe what I saw. This is ungodly!" (1984 Clemson Game)
- "Washington, thinking of Montreal and the Olympics ran out of his shoes!" (1975 Florida Game)
- "We just stepped on their face with a hobnailed boot and broke their nose. We just crushed their faces!" (2002 Tennessee Game)

___ **QUESTION 30:** He head-butted their helmets with his bald head.

Got your Meaner Than a Junkyard Dawg total? ___ / 30
So what is your Bulldogs IQ? It's time to find out!

Georgia Bulldogs IQ

Write in your scores and add up your total:

Tailgating: __ / 30

First Quarter: __ / 40

Second Quarter: __ / 40

Half Time: __ / 30

Third Quarter: __ / 40

Fourth Quarter: __ / 40

Meaner Than a Jungyard Dawg: __ / 30

Total Points: __ / 250

Got your total? Here's how it breaks down:

BULLDOGS IQ HALL OF FAME = 225 AND UP
ALL-SEC AND ALL-AMERICAN = 200-224
FOUR-YEAR LETTERMAN = 175-199
YOU MADE THE TEAM AS A WALK-ON = 150-174
YOU SHOULD HAVE GONE TO FL = 149 AND BELOW

Think you can do better next season? Well, you're going to get a shot at it—be on the lookout for Georgia Bulldogs IQ, Volume II!

About the Authors

Kim Gaddie and Keith Gaddie are alums of the University of Georgia. Kim is a community volunteer, teacher, and writer. Keith is a professor at University of Oklahoma, writer, and author of *University of Georgia Football* in the Sports by the Numbers series. When they are not hiding out at Kenny D's in Destin, at the 40 Watt in Athens, or out on Lake Burton, they and their children live in Norman, Oklahoma, with their pet junkyard dog, Vince Dooley.

Also by Keith Gaddie

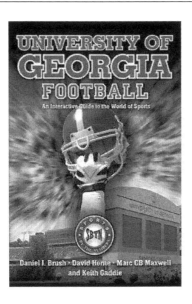

"The authors of this Sports by the Numbers book help break down the fascinating world of Georgia Football. They provide a thousand stories to satisfy the hunger and cravings of the most obsessive Bulldog fan. In the following pages, you will find facts, figures, trivia, and the history of UGA football that will either teach or remind you about why our team is the best in the country . . . You may think you are the most knowledgeable Georgia fan ever to enter the gates of Sanford Stadium, however, after just a few pages into this title, you will think otherwise. The pleasure you receive from this read will have you shouting, Gooooooo Dawgs, Sic Em!"

— Mark Nedza, President, University of Georgia G-Club

Sports by the Numbers

The award-winning Sports by the Numbers book series is a proud sponsor of Black Mesa's IQ books. SBTN is the series where every number tells a story—and whether you're a beginning fan just learning the ropes, or a diehard fanatic hanging on the outcome of every game, the crew at SBTN have got you covered.

Check out Sports by the Numbers on the web:

www.sportsbythenumbers.com

Current titles include:

- *University of Oklahoma Football*
- *University of Georgia Football*
- *Major League Baseball*
- *New York Yankees*
- *Boston Red Sox*
- *San Francisco Giants*
- *Mixed Martial Arts*
- *NASCAR*

For information about special discounts for bulk purchases, please email:

sales@savasbeatie.com

Sports by the Numbers Praise

"You think you know it all? Not so fast. To unearth fact upon fact about this historic franchise in a unique yet tangible way is an impressive feat, which is why the following pages are more than worthwhile for every member of that cult known as Red Sox Nation . . . This is a book that Red Sox fans of all ages and types will enjoy and absorb."

    — Ian Browne, Boston Red Sox Beat Writer,
    MLB.com

"Fighting is physical storytelling where villains and heroes emerge, but the back-story is what makes the sport something that persisted from B.C. times to what we know it as today. Antonio Rodrigo Nogueira living through a childhood coma only to demonstrate equal grit inside the ring on his way to two world championships. Randy Couture defying age like it was as natural as sunrise on his way to six world championships. The achievements are endless in nature, but thanks to this book, these great human narratives are translated into a universal language— numbers—in a universal medium—fighting."

    — Danny Acosta, Sherdog.com and *Fight!* Magazine
    Writer

"Statistics have long been resigned to slower, contemplative sports. Finally, they get a crack at the world's fastest sport in this fascinating piece of MMA analysis."

    — Ben Zeidler, CagePotato.com, *Fight!* Magazine

"Long-time Sooner fans will revel in the flood of memories that flow from these pages. You'll think back to a defining moment—that favorite player, an afternoon next to the radio, or that special day at Owen Field. And the information contained here is so thorough that you'll relive those memories many times."
   — Bob Stoops, Head Coach, University of Oklahoma Football

"*University of Oklahoma Football – S*ports By The Numbers is a must read for all OU Football junkies. I read trivia I didn't know or had forgotten."
   — Barry Switzer, Legendary Head Coach, University of Oklahoma Football

"Clever and insightful. For fans who don't know much about the history of stock-car racing, it's like taking the green flag."
   — Monte Dutton, best-selling NASCAR author

"You will find the most important numbers that every fan should know, like Joe DiMaggio's 56-game hitting streak, Ted Williams' .406 batting average, Hank Aaron's 755 homeruns, and Nolan Ryan's seven no-hitters, but there are hundreds of lesser-known stats. Even if you think you know everything about baseball, I guarantee you will learn a whole lot from this book."
   — Zack Hample, best-selling author of *Watching Baseball Smarter*

"This book is fascinating and informative. If you love Yankees trivia, this is the reference for you."
— Jane Heller, best-selling novelist, Yankees blogger, and author of *Confessions of a She-Fan: The Course of True Love with the New York Yankees*

"This book brings you tons of info on America's best loved and most hated team—the New York Yankees . . . a great book for any age or fan of America's Game and Team. A must read."
— Phil Speranza, author of the *2000 Yankee Encyclopedia 5th edition*

"I loved this book. I could not put it down at night. This book is the perfect bedside or coffee table reading material. *New York Yankees: An Interactive Guide to the World of Sports* has a huge collection of interesting data about the entire New York Yankees history."
— Sam Hendricks, author of *Fantasy Football Guidebook* and *Fantasy Football Almanac 2009*

"The Yankees matter—but you already knew that, and soon, you will dive into this wonderful yield by the good folks at Sports by the Numbers and you will lose yourself in baseball, in history, in numbers, and in the New York Yankees. I envy you. I can't think of a better way to pass the next couple of hours."
— Mike Vaccaro, best-selling author and award-winning columnist for the *New York Post*

Black Mesa Titles

Look for these other titles in the IQ Series:

- *Mixed Martial Arts*
- *Atlanta Braves*
- *Boston Red Sox*
- *New York Yankees*
- *Cincinnati Reds*
- *Milwaukee Brewers*
- *St. Louis Cardinals*
- *University of Oklahoma Football*
- *University of Florida Football*
- *Penn State Football*
- *San Francisco 49ers*
- *Boston Celtics*

Look for your favorite MLB and collegiate teams in Black Mesa's *If I was the Bat Boy* series, and look for your favorite NFL and collegiate teams in Black Mesa's *How to Build the Perfect Player* series, both by award-winning artist and author Cameron Silver.

For information about special discounts for bulk purchases, please email:

black.mesa.publishing@gmail.com

Praise for MMA IQ

"Every time I work on a cut I am being tested and I feel confident I can pass the test. After reading MMA IQ I'm not so sure I can do the same with this book."
— UFC Cutman Jacob "Stitch" Duran,
www.stitchdurangear.com

"MMA fans everywhere pay attention—this is your best chance to reign supreme in your favorite bar stool. The trivia and stories come at you so fast and so furious you'll wish Stitch Duran was in your corner getting you ready to do battle."
— Sam Hendricks, award-winning author of
Fantasy Football Tips: 201 Ways to Win through Player Rankings, Cheat Sheets and Better Drafting

"From the rookie fan to the pound for pound trivia champs, MMA IQ has something that will challenge the wide spectrum of fans that follow the sport."
— Robert Joyner, www.mmapayout.com

"I thought I knew MMA, but this book took my MMA IQ to a whole new level . . . fun read, highly recommended."
— William Li, www.findmmagym.com

You can visit *Mixed Martial Arts IQ* author Zac Robinson on the web:

www.sportsbythenumbersmma.com
www.cutmanstitchduran.com

Praise for NY Yankees IQ

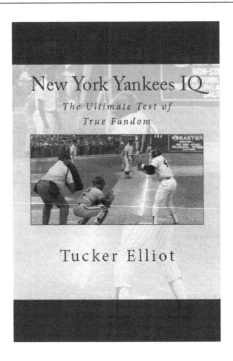

"If you consider yourself a tested veteran at baseball trivia in general or a hardcore expert at Yankees trivia in particular, it doesn't matter—you owe it to yourself to test your skills with this IQ book, because only when you pass this test can you truly claim to be a cut above everyone else."

— Daniel J. Brush, award-winning author of *New York Yankees: An Interactive Guide to the World of Sports*

Praise for Atlanta Braves IQ

"There are just two Hall of Famers who really know the Braves road from Boston to Milwaukee to Atlanta—Eddie Mathews and Braves IQ! This book will determine if you can win fourteen-straight division titles or if you will get lost trying to get off I-285. If you're a Braves fan or you know a Braves fan, this is a must-have."

— Dr. Keith Gaddie, award-winning broadcast journalist and author of *University of Georgia Football: An Interactive Guide to the World of Sports*

Made in the USA
Columbia, SC
18 December 2019